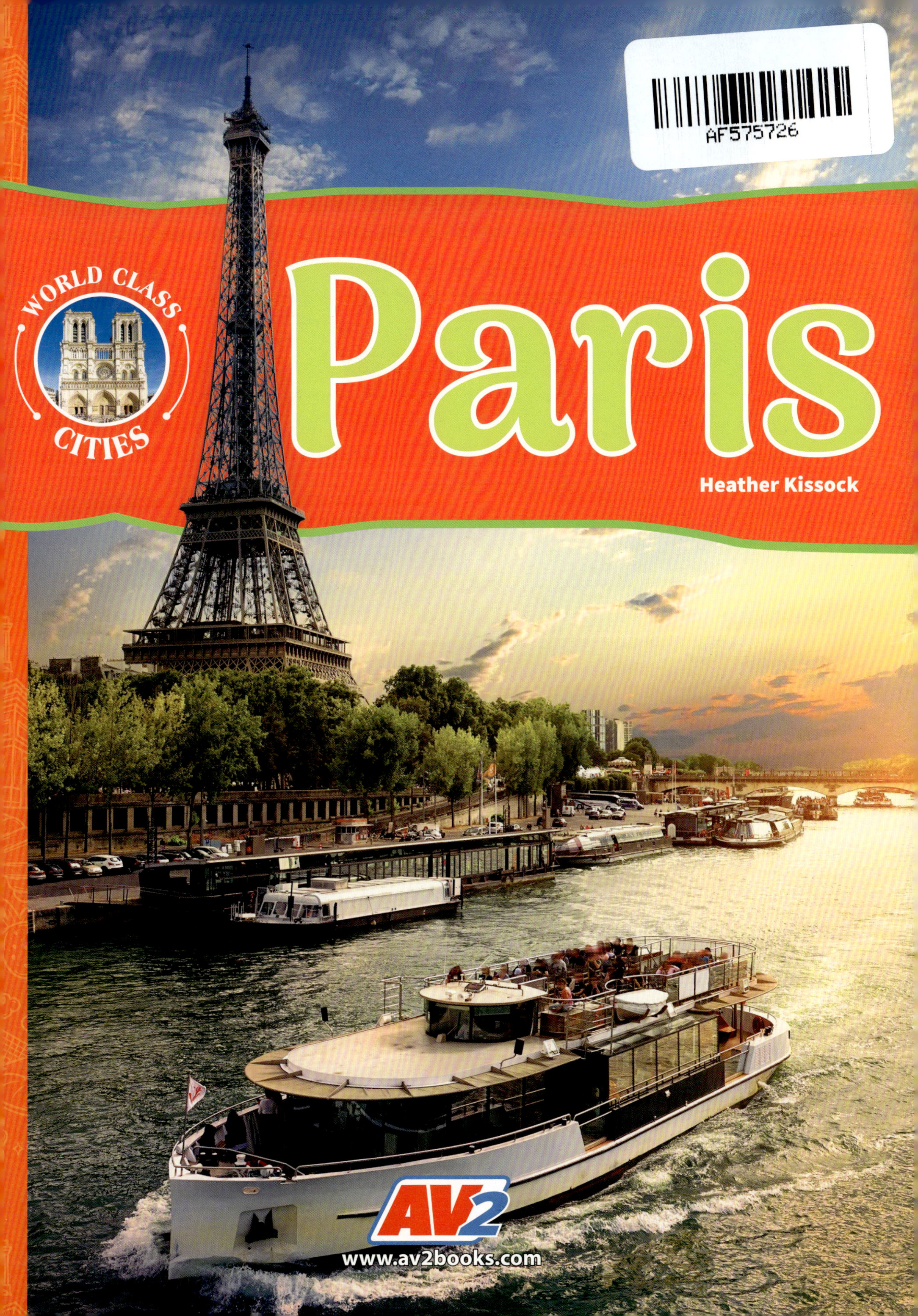
AF575726
WORLD CLASS
CITIES
Paris
Heather Kissock
AV2
www.av2books.com

Step 1
Go to **www.av2books.com**

Step 2
Enter this unique code
PCQJEV1UX

Step 3
Explore your interactive eBook!

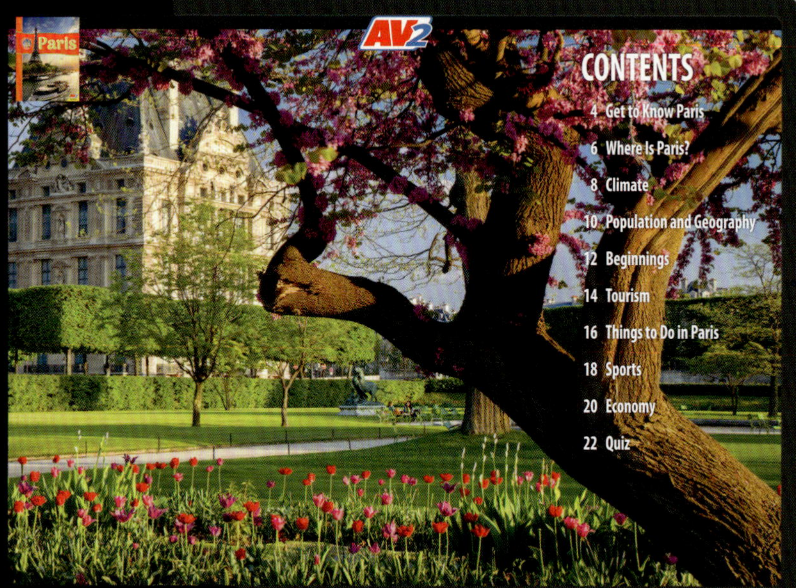

AV2 is optimized for use on any device

Your interactive eBook comes with...

Contents
Browse a live contents page to easily navigate through resources

Audio
Listen to sections of the book read aloud

Videos
Watch informative video clips

Weblinks
Gain additional information for research

Try This!
Complete activities and hands-on experiments

Key Words
Study vocabulary, and complete a matching word activity

Quizzes
Test your knowledge

Slideshows
View images and captions

This title is part of our AV2 digital subscription

1-Year 3–8 Subscription
ISBN 978-1-7911-3306-1

Access hundreds of AV2 titles with our digital subscription.
Sign up for a FREE trial at **www.av2books.com/trial**

Paris

Contents

Get to Know Paris

Paris is the capital city of a country called France. It is also known as the "City of Light." Many of Paris's **landmarks** are lit up at night. The Eiffel Tower alone has 20,000 light bulbs.

Comparing World Towers

Where Is Paris?

Paris is located in north-central France. The country sits on the western edge of the **continent** of Europe. The Atlantic Ocean makes up France's western border. Three countries and a sea lie to the south. France shares its eastern border with five other countries.

There are many places to visit in France. Some people come to experience the country's history. They go to castles and churches. Others want to relax on beaches along the coast. Many head to the mountains to ski and hike.

Words to Know

Most people in France speak French.
See if you can say a few words in this language.

Climate

Paris has a mild **climate**. Summers are mostly warm and sunny. Winters can be cold and windy.

Rain can fall at any time of year. Showers may appear suddenly and be over in a few minutes. Snow sometimes falls in the winter. It does not stay on the ground for long.

A Year in Paris

Average Summer Temperature
72° Fahrenheit (22° Celsius)

Average Winter Temperature
50° Fahrenheit (10°C)

Average Annual Rainfall
25.1 inches (637 millimeters)

Population and Geography

More than 2 million people live in Paris. Another 10 million live in the area around the city. This makes Paris the largest city in France.

Paris was built along the Seine River. At 482 miles (776 kilometers) in length, the Seine is one of France's longest rivers. The river holds three islands. The largest island is called Île de la Cité.

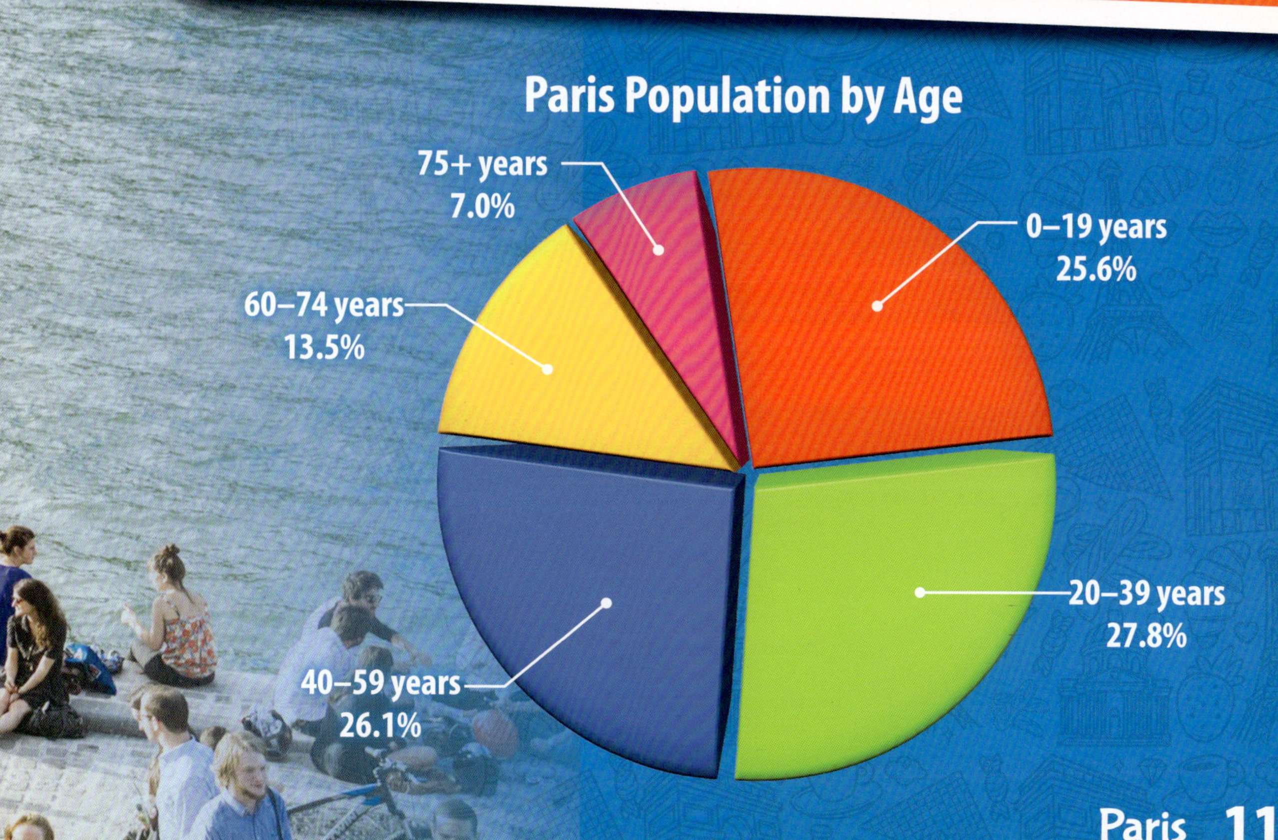

Beginnings

People were living in this part of France at least 9,000 years ago. Over time, a group called the **Parisii** formed a village in the area. In about 52 BC, the **Romans** arrived. They invaded the village and made it their own. The village became known as Paris.

In 508 AD, the **Franks** took control of Paris. Their king made it the capital of his **empire**. Other rulers followed. Some of them made other cities the capital. In 1944, Paris became France's capital for good.

Paris Timeline

Paris has been the site of many important events over the years. All have made the city what it is today.

2,300 years ago

The Parisii form a settlement in what is now Paris.

508 AD

Clovis, King of the Franks, makes Paris his capital.

1789

Paris becomes the center of the **French Revolution.**

1889

The Eiffel Tower is completed in time for the Paris World Fair.

1940

The Germans take control of Paris during World War II.

2019

A fire destroys much of the Notre-Dame de Paris cathedral.

Tourism

Many people come to Paris for its art. The city is home to the world's largest art museum. The Louvre was once a royal palace. Today, it houses more than 300,000 works of art.

Another palace also draws visitors to Paris. The Palace of Versailles was built in the 1600s for the French king. With 2,300 rooms, 1,250 chimneys, and 67 staircases, it is one of the grandest palaces in the world.

Things to Do in Paris

Notre-Dame de Paris
Located on Île de la Cité, this cathedral is one of Paris's best-known landmarks. Its **Gothic** style attracts visitors from around the world.

Champs-Élysées
Stretching for more than 1 mile (1.6 km), this street is often called the "world's most beautiful avenue." More than 300,000 people visit the Champs-Élysées every day to take in its many shops and cafés.

Arc de Triomphe

This monument was built in the 1800s to honor those who fought for France. It rises 164 feet (50 m) above the Champs-Élysées.

Paris Zoological Park

This zoo has been open since 1934. Today, it covers 37 acres (15 hectares) and is home to thousands of animals.

Musée d'Orsay

This art museum is located in an old train station. It holds some of the world's best-known artworks.

ŠKODA
ŠKODA
BORA

Sports

Soccer is a popular sport in Paris. The city is home to four soccer teams. Paris Saint-Germain is the city's best-known team. They play out of the Parc des Princes stadium. This stadium can hold about 48,000 people.

In the spring, people come to Paris to watch the French Open. This tennis tournament brings the world's top-ranking players to the city. The Tour de France is another important event. The finish line for this bicycle race is on the Champs-Élysées.

Economy

Tourism is the top **industry** in Paris. Every year, more than 40 million people visit the city. They stay in hotels, eat at restaurants, and tour attractions.

Paris is also known as a business center. It is home to some of the world's largest companies. The city also has some of the largest banks in Europe.

Paris's Top 5 Visitors by Country

1. United Kingdom

2. United States
3. Germany
4. Italy
5. China

ZARA
HOME

Quiz

1 Paris is the capital city of which country?

ANSWER: France

2 By what other name is Paris known?

ANSWER: The "City of Light"

3 Along what river was Paris built?

ANSWER: The Seine River

4 In what year was the Eiffel Tower completed?

ANSWER: 1889

5 How many works of art are housed at the Louvre?

ANSWER: More than 300,000

6 In what part of Paris is the Notre-Dame de Paris cathedral located?

ANSWER: Île de la Cité

7 Which major cycling race ends on the Champs-Élysées?

ANSWER: The Tour de France

8 How many people visit Paris each year?

ANSWER: More than 40 million

Key Words

climate: the average weather conditions of a region throughout a year

continent: one of seven large land areas on Earth

empire: a group of countries, lands, or peoples under one government or ruler

Franks: a group of people that came from central Europe to settle in what is now France

French Revolution: a period of time in France when the people of France overthrew the king and took control of the government

Gothic: a style of architecture that features tall pillars, curved ceilings, and pointed arches

industry: a branch of business, trade, or manufacturing

islet: a small island

landmarks: important buildings, structures, or places

Parisii: an ancient people that lived along the Seine River during the Iron Age

Romans: people who lived in or came from ancient Rome

Index

Get the best of both worlds.

AV2 bridges the gap between print and digital.

The expandable resources toolbar enables quick access to content including **videos**, **audio**, **activities**, **weblinks**, **slideshows**, **quizzes**, and **key words**.

Animated videos make static images come alive.

Resource icons on each page help readers to further **explore key concepts**.

Published by AV2
276 5th Avenue, Suite 704 #917
New York, NY 10001
Website: www.av2books.com

Library of Congress Cataloging-in-Publication Data
Names: Kissock, Heather, author.
Title: Paris / Heather Kissock.
Description: New York, NY : AV2, 2022. | Series: World class cities | Includes index. | Audience: Ages 8-11 | Audience: Grades 2-3
Identifiers: LCCN 2021003463 (print) | LCCN 2021003464 (ebook) | ISBN 9781791138301 (library binding) | ISBN 9781791138318 (paperback) | ISBN 9781791138325
Subjects: LCSH: Paris (France)--Juvenile literature.
Classification: LCC DC707 .K53 2022 (print) | LCC DC707 (ebook) | DDC 944/.361--dc23
LC record available at https://lccn.loc.gov/2021003463
LC ebook record available at https://lccn.loc.gov/2021003464

Printed in Guangzhou, China
1 2 3 4 5 6 7 8 9 0 25 24 23 22 21

022021
101120

Project Coordinator: Heather Kissock
Designer: Ana María Vidal

Every reasonable effort has been made to trace ownership and to obtain permission to reprint copyright material. The publishers would be pleased to have any errors or omissions brought to their attention so that they may be corrected in subsequent printings.

AV2 acknowledges Getty Images, Alamy, and Newscom as its primary image suppliers for this title.